AF769798

CONTEXT FOR A CUBAN TRANSITION:

An argument in favor of democracy and a market economy

COLECCIÓN CUBA Y SUS JUECES

EDICIONES UNIVERSAL, Miami Florida, 2004

Ernesto F. Betancourt

CONTEXT FOR A CUBAN TRANSITION:

An argument in favor of democracy and a market economy

...EDICIONES UNIVERSAL

Copyright © 2004 by Ernesto F. Betancourt & TEDA Corp.

First Edition, 2004

EDICIONES UNIVERSAL
P.O. Box 450353 (Shenandoah Station)
Miami, FL 33245-0353. USA
Tel: (305) 642-3234 Fax: (305) 642-7978
e-mail: ediciones@ediciones.com
http://www.ediciones.com

Library of Congress Catalog Card No.: 2004100396
I.S.B.N.: 1-59388-022-7

Text Design: Luis García Fresquet

Cover Design: Luis García Fresquet

Todos los derechos
son reservados. Ninguna parte de
este libro puede ser reproducida o transmitida
en ninguna forma o por ningún medio electrónico o mecánico,
incluyendo fotocopiadoras, grabadoras o sistemas computarizados,
sin el permiso por escrito del autor, excepto en el caso de
breves citas incorporadas en artículos críticos o en
revistas. Para obtener información diríjase a
Ediciones Universal.

TABLE OF CONTENTS

INTRODUCTION

It has been argued that, after Castro, Cuba is doomed to a life of tyranny and little development under a succession, rather than a transition to a free and democratic society made prosperous by a market economy.

In fact, the American military, influenced by the analysis of Castro's spy Ana Belén Montes, have been sponsoring a Raúl Castro succession. This results from the same cultural blindness and organizational arrogance that led the Pentagon to sponsor the Bay of Pigs with total disregard for the historic situation at the time, in particular the mood of the Cuban people. At that time, they underestimated the consequences of their actions and of the stranglehold Castro had over Cuban public opinion. Now, that same cultural blindness and organizational arrogance, is leading them to ignore the hopes and aspirations of the Cuban people. This time they are overestimating Castro's stranglehold over Cuban public opinion.

I totally reject such a dire future for the Cuban people. In this monograph, an analysis will be made of the current public opinion dynamics of Cuban society using the model I developed to evaluate revolutionary propensity during four decades of involvement in the Cuban revolution. The model emerged from that experience.

In the Appendix I describe the evolution of the methodology I developed over the years, ending with the publication of *Revolutionary Strategy: A Handbook for Practitioners*.

Consistent with the approach developed in that book, we will argue the case for a transition, instead of a succession, based on the impact of the contemporary context of Cuban public opinion. After briefly defining the present spectrum of Cuban public opinion, the first section will consider the external environment and the decline of Castro's international image, a key factor in determining his charismatic stranglehold over followers and opponents alike.

This section covers the impact on Cuban public opinion of the following external events: the collapse of the Soviet Bloc, both in terms of ideology and economic support, the Pope's visit, the expansion of neoliberalism and globalization, with its complementary political freedom and democracy, the 9/11 attack and the war on terrorism, including Iraq and Afghanistan, Venezuela, the European reaction to Castro's repression of the dissidence and the emergence of a democratic left alternative in Latin America. The cumulative impact of these events has eroded Castro's charismatic hold over Cuba and divided the regime, making a Raúl succession less feasible.

Next, there is an analysis of the evolution of the spectrum of Cuban public opinion as a result of the following internal events: dollarization, economic reforms (including the collapse of the sugar industry and the expansion of tourism), emergence of the dissidence, the Elian case, the Proyecto Varela, and the Miami trial of Cuban spies. The cumulative impact of the internal events has ended the equalitarian appeal of the regime and led to the emergence of a dissidence that can be repressed but not finished.

Then, the feasibility of various outcomes will be considered in the light of the trends in public opinion identified. The possible outcomes include a US intervention, a coup, a civil war, a succession and a negotiated transition. We start from the assumption that a stable solution requires that it satisfies the interests of all stakeholders involved in the Cuban situation. The conclusion is that Cuba has reached a point when it is ready for a transition restoring democratic rule and a market economy based on a massive privatization of the means of production.

Finally, drawing on the experience of the systemic transitions in the former Soviet Bloc, consideration will be given to the assistance that may be required from various external sources to ensure a successful transition.

I

CURRENT SPECTRUM OF CUBAN PUBLIC OPINION

Public opinion is very difficult to gauge in a society in which prevails what Cubans call the "double moral," that is, hiding what you really think. Facing a regime that has refined the art of repression to incredible extremes, Cubans are what we may call well adjusted schizophrenics. To survive they develop the skill to avoid expressing their real thoughts. This starts early in life, when the family tells children not to repeat at school, or when playing, what they hear at home in family conversations. The growth of the dissidence and the easily observed willingness of people to speak critically of the miserable reality they face in their lives are indications that this double moral has weakened substantially in the last decade.

As the model guiding this monograph states, public opinion for purposes of revolutionary potential is divided along a spectrum going from segments willing to resort to violence to defend the status quo to those willing to resort to violence to overthrow it, including those willing to endure repression as a passive manifestation of their opposition to the status quo. Those are segments "A" and "E" respectively. In between, we have those who only support the status quo peacefully, segment "B", and those who also oppose it peacefully, segment "D". Finally, we have the ïndifferents or neutrals in segment "C", they are like ostriches, they just do not get involved one way or the other.

In the current situation in Cuba, **Segment A** is formed mostly by people from the MININT, that is the people of Seguridad del Estado and the National Police, with close support from the hoodlums from the various ad-hoc Brigades that are mobilized against any target selected by the Party or its affiliates in the Committees for the Defense of the Revolution (CDR) whenever it is felt that intimidation of citizens is warranted. The CDRs are ambiguous in many cases in their commitment to resort to violence. Evidence filters through of tolerance of dissidence and hesitation in supporting harassment of opponents and dissenters. For example, many people refuse to participate in the so-called "actos de repudio" against their neighbors and the regime is forced to bring the brigades that perform them from other neighborhoods. In fact, in the last wave of repression against dissidents in March, 2003, there were reports of neighbors coming out in support of those being arrested, something that had not happened before.

In theory, the MINFAR is supposed to be part of **Segment A**. They are the military on whom the regime relies for firepower to protect itself, the ultimate group in being committed to resort to violence to defend the status quo. In most of Latin America there is a tradition of military involvement in civilian affairs. However, the Cuban military has a different tradition based on Soviet military doctrine, in which the Party is the one, through the security apparatus, that handles internal order, with the military focusing on national defense. In addition, during the alliance with the Soviet Union, the Cuban military became the standard bearer of the so-called "internationalist" banner. This was a source of great national pride for the Cuban military. During that period, the military was even resentful of MININT cadres, whom they distrusted and despised.

To what extent this has changed after the Ochoa crisis is hard to determine. The fact is, however, that the military, in the person of general Abelardo Colomé Ibarra and his military collaborators, took over the MININT. At least in the eyes of the population, their prestige went down, compounded by the corruption resulting from the deliberate policy--apparently conceived by Raúl Castro--of granting them sinecures in state enterprises to ensure their loyalty a la Trujillo and Somoza. As a result, many in the military are likely to resort to violence only if they perceive their privileges threatened, with loyalty to the regime being less of a factor, while those in line commands without access to dollar privileges are more likely to be unwilling to resort to violence against the people, as in the past. Nationalism is still a powerful motivation among **Segment A**.

Segment B is formed by Party cadres, the nomenklatura and parallel mobilization organizations, such as the Committees for the Defense of the Revolution (CDRs), Cuban Workers Federation, the

Federation of Cuban Women, the Communist Youth, the ANAP, etc. Membership in these organizations is perceived as tickets to access to education, jobs, some material benefits and, of course, power. Since the role of these organizations is not predicated on resort to violence, many members are basically opportunists who would try to come on top in any new situation that emerges without being willing to resort to violence unless directly threatened. However, membership in the CDRs may reflect more a commitment to **Segment A** than to **Segment B**. The majority of the cadres in this segment are aware that the Communist ideology has failed all over the world. Others may pay only lip service to it, but consider their interests demand they support the regime. However, either out of conviction or due to their basic interests and privileges, they all are still likely to respond to regime nationalists appeals.

Segment C is the one that has grown the most. It is fed by two powerful forces: one, the despair of people who have reached the conclusion that the repressive apparatus makes opposition impossible; and, the other, the cynicism of true believers who, all of the sudden, become disenchanted with the regime and vent their frustration in a sea of disbelief and impotence. This is the segment from which most of the participants in the visa lottery and the suicidal rafters come. Others fall into a state of anomie. They are dropouts from any struggle. Escape, legally, without any risk, or illegally, at great risk, seems a way out for many in this segment. The other alternative is passivity and indifference, mere survival. To struggle is futile. **Segment C**, at present, is probably the most substantial proportion of the population. Nationalism evokes a weak response within this segment. Although this may offend diehard nationalists, in their despair and/or cynicism, people in this segment probably are the most receptive to the idea of annexation.

Segment D includes those who are more likely to defy the rules established by the regime. Their opposition to the status quo is manifested in violating those rules to engage in illegal activities or to take advantage of any lessening of controls to undertake self employment initiatives. They also include many of those engaged in independent libraries and agricultural cooperatives or similar efforts that depend on one's own wits rather than on what the government grants. Recipients of remittances are likely to move within this segment since they do not rely on the government for their survival and that makes them more independent, although some of them are likely to be in segment C precisely for fear of losing that privilege. The Catholic Church is increasingly taking a position of challenging the regime and, through groups like the one in Pinar del Río that publishes the magazine VITRAL, is articulating and disseminating an alternative ideology to the official one. **Segment D** includes already several million people and is the breeding ground for a market economy within Cuban society.

Segment E is very small at present in Cuba, probably in the tens of thousands, although it has grown tremendously during the last decade and, despite government repression, continues to survive. So far, it is limited to those willing to endure government repression by defying the regime, the overwhelming repressive capacity of the regime makes resort to violence against the status quo totally unfeasible. Besides the thousands who participate in openly dissident organizations of journalists, lawyers, doctors, teachers, and other professionals, it includes the thousands who were willing to sign the ProyectoVarela petition and many in prison.

II

IMPACT OF EXTERNAL EVENTS

The external events that provide the international context for our analysis include: the collapse of the Soviet Bloc, both in terms of ideology and economic support, the Pope's visit, the expansion of neo-liberalism and globalization, with its complementary political freedom and democracy, the 9/11 attack and the war on terrorism, including Iraq and Afghanistan, Venezuela, the European reaction to Castro's repression of the dissidence and the emergence of a democratic left alternative in Latin America.

The **collapse of the Soviet Bloc** was an abysmal policy failure for Castro, depriving him of a coherent ideology with which to dress up his Caribbean caudillo regime, it also put an end to Cuba's military internationalism and caused the loss of massive economic support, to the tune of several billion dollars a year, in subsidized markets for Cuban sugar and supply of oil below market prices. This was what is called a trigger event.

Within those willing to resort to force to support the regime, the military (MINFAR) and the security apparatus (MININT), the collapse of the Soviet Bloc weakened tremendously their privileged status due to budget cuts and it diluted their ideological justification, military internationalism came to an end, forcing a massive reduction in the armed forces and the credibility of the eventual victory of communism over capitalism lost its effectiveness as an ideological appeal. The regime was forced to retain the loyalty of these cadres through giving them sinecures as part of the military enterprise oligarchy conceived by Raúl Castro.

A similar impact took place among those willing to support the regime peacefully, mostly members of the Party and mobilization entities who saw their well being reduced and the ideological underpinnings of the regime weakened. However, most were not included in the military entrepreneur group. The economic collapse led to the so-called Special Period austerity measures and eventually the limited reforms, dollarization, opening the economy to foreign investors, creating the semi-private agricultural cooperatives and the so-called cuentapropistas. The Special Period may have led many in this segment drift to the cynically indifferent C center segment, which expanded significantly.

Some among those supporting the status quo peacefully in segment B may have gone past the center into taking a more critical questioning position of discrete quiet opposition from which the most unhappy moved into those in the dissidence. The emergence of the dissidence that had been fed by the availability of access to free information in the form of Radio Martí broadcasts, was probably reinforced by these events in the Soviet Bloc. In the absence of such independent sources of information, the regime would have been able to reduce its impact more effectively.

The unquestionable repressive capacity of the state discouraged resort to open violence in defiance of the regime and, as a result, no segment emerged willing to resort to violence to overthrow the regime. Even so, the Malecón riots in 1994 reflect a potential for violence underpinning the apparent quiet.

The impact of **the Pope's visit** is more limited in scope; however, it has been highly significant in terms of the attitudes of the population as a whole. This visit was under negotiation from 1987 to 1998, and the main argument centered on the extent of the visit. Castro just wanted a Pope's stopover for photo opportunities, while the Pope insisted on being allowed to make contact with the Cuban people throughout the island. In the end, the Pope prevailed and Castro accepted to have him traveling from one end of the island to the other. At the last minute, the regime also agreed to provide access to Cuban mass media.

Castro was surprised at the degree of fervor evoked, even among Party members. As soon as this became evident to him, he started to make arrangements to control public events. The most worrisome issue for Castro emerged when the Pope told the Cubans not to be afraid. This really aimed at one of the underpinnings of regime control. That is why, on the day of the Pope's departure, Castro decided to confront the Pope on this issue and told him openly that, in Cuba nobody was afraid. As soon as the Pope departed, the regime started a campaign that was called "the depopification campaign."

Over the years, the impact of the visit has been diluted, including the concessions initially made to the Catholic Church, as has been acknowledged by leaders of the hierarchy on more than one occasion. However, many Cubans decided to follow the Pope's advice, as Castro feared, and started to lose fear of repression. This has resulted in an increased displacement of attitudes away from passivity that has fed the dissidence growth. Therefore, the greatest impact has been on the peaceful opposition and the emergence of issues such as the Proyecto Varela. The willingness to sign and give your address and identity number in a petition to be submitted to regime authorities is an act of courage that would not have found thousands of willing citizens had it not been because of the Pope's encouragement to lose fear.

The collapse of Communism was a victory for democracy and capitalism as alternative ways of organizing social relations. Initially, it did not have too much of an ideological impact, the West was not really prepared to exploit this surprising development. However, slowly, it led into the emergence of **neo-liberal economic policies and globalization** as the prevailing criteria for worldwide economic growth. Parallel to this, the idea of **freedom and democracy** as the basis for organizing political rule gained widespread acceptance worldwide, and particularly so in the Americas. This culminated in Lima with the approval of the Democratic Charter of the Americas, precisely on September 11, 2001. Parallel to the Regional Free Trade Area, they became the two great ideological concepts which emerged to guide the region in the new century. At the same time, the failure to improve distribution of wealth has resulted in serious challenges to neo-liberalism and weakened the commitment to democracy.

The impact of these new concepts on the various segments of Cuban public opinion is not evident due to the prevailing press censorship in Cuba and the so-called "double-moral", which makes Cubans keep to themselves notions they consider could get them into trouble. However, within members of the military and security apparatus incorporated to enterprise activities, whose support is essential for regime survival, the logic of their interests is consistent with Cuba incorporating those concepts into its system. Success of their business endeavors will, to a great extent, require the compatibilization of Cuba's economic and political systems with prevailing worldwide trends and, particularly, those that have been imbedded into the Inter-American System. For example, absence of democratic rule would prevent Cuba from rejoining the OAS and, therefore, from having access to the financial resources of the Inter-American Development Bank. This explains the rabid attacks of Castro on neo-liberalism and the ALCA. He realizes the concepts and principles guiding these agencies are anathema to the type of political and economic rule he is trying to preserve in the island that, more than communistic, is feudalistic. In the case of ALCA, Castro realizes that to the extent other countries in the region join, while his regime is excluded, his isolation increases.

The impact of these issues will be felt with greater intensity among segments A and B, groups willing to support the status quo either by resorting to violence or peacefully, the moment Castro's charisma is out of the picture. The willingness to resort to violence to defend the status quo, in particular, is likely to be weakened by lack of conviction on the long run feasibility of a regime that is isolated from its neighbors. It will have little impact on the attitudes of segment C, but will certainly provide great stimulus to the growth and militancy of segments D and, perhaps, even E. This is likely to be the case in relation to workers rights, with the old tradition of union militancy, which was very strong in Cuba in the past, reawakening itself very early, once workers realize they have to fight to protect their rights.

The **9/11 attack and the war on terrorism** completely changed the international environment. Castro, who had been a long time advocate and practitioner of terrorism in his foreign policy, realized immediately that he had to place some distance between such activities and Cuba, although his previous entanglements were too deep and complicated to discard totally. **Iraq and Afghanistan** are blunt reminders that the new US policy of preemptive war for harboring terrorist could result in lightning retaliation if Castro supported groups were to undertake any operations against the US. This is an option that Castro had reserved for himself if he decided to end his career bringing Cuba down in flames by provoking a US intervention.

If anything, Osama bin Laden must be the target of great envy and resentment on the part of Castro. By being the first one who caused substantial loss of life and destruction of property in the continental US, bin Laden preempted a historic event that Castro had in mind for his grand finale. With his tremendous capacity for maneuvering, Castro immediately changed his tune on terrorism, even offering landing rights to US planes and, when the Taliban prison was built in Guantánamo, he accepted that use –after some hesitation to calm his followers– and even offered to provide medical services for the inmates.

Cuba promptly ratified all UN treaties on terrorism. It is also evident Castro stopped, at least for the time being, those potential terrorist activities which could result in embarrassing revelations. For example, the Petis camps One and Two used for training revolutionaries from all over the world in terrorist operations, are reported to be still open, although no information is available about who is using them. They were established in Pinar del Río in the 1960s and were used by all groups, from the Palestinian PLO to the FARC and M-19 from Colombia, the Uruguayan Tupamaros and Chileans from the MIR and the Manuel Rodríguez Front, as well as Che's infiltrators in Bolivia, not to mention Central American guerrillas from the Sandinistas and the FMLN.

As part of what he labeled the Biological Front, Castro had installed BSL-4 level equipment at the biotechnology laboratories, which could be used to produce biological material for weapons. This equipment was turned inactive, although they have not been dismantled, as a recent report released by the Defense Information Center reveals. This report does not give any explanation of why the BSL-4 equipment was installed in the first place. On August 23, 2002, *Granma* even had the nerve of making a formal offer from Castro's government to provide assistance to the US with its technical competence in relation to the West Nile virus epidemic. There are strong indications that this epidemic may have been generated from Cuba using migratory birds for its propagation.

Another example, the interference with ARINC, the Air Control Traffic System Radio Network at US airports, frequently made since 1985 using the 1500 KW transmitters provided by the Soviet Union under the Titan plan, has been stopped. Although there is a report of such interference at New York airports from the FCC HFDF Center, as recently as 5/13/99. Needless to say that airport radio interference was a potential form of terrorism that could have produced disastrous air clashes at US airports. In fact, Soviet generals complained to Raúl Castro on several occasions of such an incident leading to a conflict with the US.

The impact of these sudden Castro terrorism policy reversals on the different segments of Cuban public opinion are limited, since terrorist promotion activities are carried under strict compartmentalization rules and, therefore, they are not a matter of knowledge beyond the limited circle of people involved. Since the US also clamps down on any public information on such activities, to avoid public opinion pressure to take remedial action, there is little public awareness of what is going on. However, among those in the know within segment A from the MINFAR and the MININT, these policy reversals must have awakened concerns as to the dangers Cuba has been incurring from engaging in such activities. To that extent, they may become skeptical about the wisdom of engaging in them to start with.

Venezuela is another external event we will consider in this analysis. The triumph of Hugo Chávez brought to Castro a gift from the gods. Here was a country rich in oil that fell on his lap out of the blue sky. There were two benefits to Castro from this situation. One was the abject adulation of Chávez for him, this reinforced his charismatic appeal as a successful international figure, one of the centerpieces of Castro's rule, particularly among members of the armed forces and the security apparatus. And, second, the economic windfall of having access to oil without having to pay for it.

An unintended consequence of Chávez subordination to Castro is the alienation of the majority of the Venezuelan people to a degree that Chávez' fate--should his mandate be revoked, as seems very likely--could be very damaging to the Castro regime in both respects. Therefore, Castro is getting more entangled every day, although at the time of this writing there are some signals that Castro may be trying to limit his losses and eventually betray Chávez, provided he can preserve the oil supply.

Again, the impact on Cuba so far has been limited to segments A and B and it has been favorable to Castro, reinforcing his charismatic hold over his inner circle and providing substantial financial resources in addition. However, should the Venezuelan outcome be the peaceful revocation of Chávez mandate, particularly, if the OAS Democratic Charter is invoked in the final stage--which is quite likely--the impact on Castro's hold in power would be devastating. His charisma will be severely weakened, the economy will take a strong turn for the worse and the Cuban people in all segments will have the example of a society ridding itself of a populist dictator in a democratic fashion.

Among segments A and B, the collapse of Chávez will provoke a serious questioning of Castro's leadership and therefore their willingness to resort to violence and provide peaceful support to preserve the status quo will be severely reduced. Economically, the new oligarchy of military entrepreneurs will not be happy with the consequences of losing free oil supplies for an economy already touching bottom. Segment C will probably grow with some of the disenchanted from segments A and B. However, the peaceful opposition in segment D and the dissidence bridging between segments D and E will get a great boost. Not only will the present regional commitment to democracy, as one of the accepted principles for the Inter-American System, would receive a dramatic boost, but it would have been successfully applied in a country very close to Cuba.

The **European reaction to Castro's repression of the dissidence** has surprised the regime leadership and its followers. This move was made by Castro simultaneously with the Iraq invasion in the belief that the world's attention would be focused on the Middle East. The European Union is committed to democracy and, even more so, against the death penalty, to an extent underestimated by Castro. The European democratic left has joined conservative groups in criticizing Castro over his repressive actions.

Castro's response in withdrawing the application to the Cotonú Agreement to receive economic assistance from the Europeans, has significant costs to Cuba in terms of loss of tariff free access to markets and sharing in the financial assistance offered from a pool of around 13 billion dollars. The petty sanctions of withdrawing diplomatic access to Cuban offices to European Union embassies in Havana could seriously impair their ability to assist their tourists visiting Cuba. In the long run, this may result in a reduction of traffic from the most important source of tourism to Cuba. This, at a time when efforts to open the US tourist market have failed due to the Bush veto threat and it is unlikely they could be revived until after the US 2004 elections.

The impact of this event on the various segments of Cuban public opinion has not manifested itself publicly. Within segments A and B, the fact that Cuba is further isolated would not increase their confidence in the leadership, therefore this will weaken Castro's charismatic hold over his supporters in these segments. The raising of the threat of an American invasion is probably a Castro public relations gimmick to offset that reaction. Appeals to nationalism are wearing thin, mostly due to their lack of credibility. More so from a regime that is frantically trying to increase its economic dependency on the US as a source of food supplies and tourist income.

The military entrepreneurs do not express themselves openly but they are the source of all kind of rumors reflecting increasing stress within regime supporters. The most striking manifestation of this stress is the campaign to discredit Elizardo Sánchez Santa Cruz, with the accusation of his being a regime agent infiltrated in the dissidence. The attack failed because people realized there was something fishy in the regime denouncing one of its own agents. More likely, this was an effort to weaken a faction within the regime that somehow was supportive of Mr. Sánchez.

If anything, this attack revealed how weak is Castro's control over his regime. Back in 1989, when faced with similar dissent within his regime, he got rid of general Arnaldo Ochoa in just two months. Now, the dissenting forces within the military establishment are too many and too heavily entrenched to be handled in such an expeditious fashion. The commitment to resort to violence to support the status quo, the basic role of segment A, seems to be much weaker today. And, the same may be said of segment B.

Finally, **the emergence of the democratic left in Latin America** is another event already having an impact on Cuban public opinion. Castro exploited to his advantage the electoral victories of Lula in

Brazil and Kirchner in Argentina. The visit to attend the inauguration of Kirchner in Argentina was an unquestionable public relations success that reinforced Castro's charismatic hold in Cuba. To a lesser extent, the electoral victories in Paraguay and Ecuador have also been a source of encouragement and the forced resignation of the President of Bolivia is also an encouraging event for Castro. Ironically, at a time that the democratic left worldwide was breaking with Castro--the Portuguese writer Saramago statement that he could not continue supporting him comes to mind—Latin America seemed to go in a totally different direction.

Under these circumstances, one would have expected Castro to attend the Iberoamerican Summit in Santa Cruz de la Sierra, Bolivia. Yet, at the last minute he cancelled his attendance, sending the colorless figure of Carlos Lage in his place. For the third year in a row Castro was not able to cavort with his fellow presidents of the Americas. Missing such an opportunity was definitely a setback for Castro.

More so, since he had been invited by Evo Morales, the Bolivian cocalero leader who engineered the overthrow of President Sánchez de Losada in Bolivia to attend the Cumbre Alternativa, to take place simultaneously, jointly with Lula, Kirchner and Chávez in order to launch a political movement of the left in Latin America "to challenge the US with a new VietNam." Those were his exact words.

Lula, under pressure from political moderates in Brasil, openly announced he had no intention to attend the Cumbre Alternativa, although he attended the Cumbre Iberoamericana. Kirchner initially announced he was too busy to attend, although after he realized that neither Lula nor Castro were attending the Cumbre Alternativa, was able to promptly clear his agenda to attend the Cumbre Iberoamericana. Only Chávez attended Evo Morales' Cumbre Alternativa.

A cruel truth is hitting Castro, the success of the democratic left in attaining power in Latin America is having a sobering impact on the loose anti-American rhetoric he uses and expects them to follow once in power. These leaders realize that they have to moderate themselves in order to govern within democratic rules of the game and that, no matter how much they question neo-liberalism, they have to pursue reasonable economic policies to try to ensure monetary stability and payment of their foreign debt.

Under this climate, Castro is becoming obsolete to his friends and will increasingly be less able to rely on their support for his rabid anti-American policies. A week after the Cumbre Iberoamericana, the meeting in Miami to discuss the implementation of the ALCA, the free trading zone for the Americas, took place. Contrary to Castro's expectations, the meeting was not a failure. On the contrary, facing the reality of the extreme diversity of situations to be reconciled, the US agreed to a more realistic approach and the work will proceed mostly through bilateral agreements. Chile has already finalized its agreement and Central America is very advanced in the negotiations. The Dominican Republic and Panama are likely to be incorporated to the Central American agreement and all the Andean countries, except Venezuela, are in the process of starting their negotiations.

Again, little is known about the reaction of the various segments of Cuban public opinion to this situation. However, a very painful fact is emerging clearly, Cuba is the only country in the whole Hemisphere whose enterprises are not getting reoriented and retooled to participate in this regional market. The oligarchs of the military enterprises, with strong links to segments A and B within the regime, and their foreign partners in mixed enterprises, cannot be totally ignorant of the implications for their businesses of this isolation. Every day, the present status quo in Cuba becomes less worthy of being supported, either peacefully or violently.

III

IMPACT OF INTERNAL EVENTS

In this chapter we will consider the impact on the attitudes of the various sectors of the population of selected internal events. Among the events selected are: dollarization, economic reforms (including the collapse of the sugar industry and the expansion of tourism), emergence of the dissidence, the Elian case, the Proyecto Varela, and the Miami trial of Cuban spies.

In response to the loss of Soviet Bloc subsidies, the regime undertook a series of measures under the banner of the Special Period in Times of Peace. Cuba's GDP decreased around 35 to 40 percent and a big share of Cuba's foreign trade had to be shifted on short notice. The rationing card that before offered a floor for equal access to food, cosmetics and other consumer items is unable to assure more than a couple of weeks of inadequate supply, forcing people to resort to non-rationed sources at higher prices, including in dollars. In addition to the ideological disaster implicit in the failure of the Communist system, the severe decline in the standard of living has been very demoralizing.

In his speech on July 26, 1993, Castro announced that circulation of the dollar was no longer illegal. This move is what we call **dollarization**. In doing so, Castro acknowledged that this was necessary due to the fact that to imprison every citizen holding dollars could become a task exceeding the capabilities of the Cuban police. Once the holding of dollars became legal, remittances from relatives overseas started to grow until it is claimed to be the biggest source of net foreign exchange for the country.

We should take those claims with a grain of salt. The amount of remittances has been reported at a level of more than one billion dollars. However, such claims seem to mix actual emigrant remittances with other sources the government is hiding, one of which is likely to be money laundering. A small calculation will demonstrate the unfeasibility of these magnitudes for remittances only.

For that much money to be remitted, 400,000 emigrants would have to be sending regularly $2,500 a year to their relatives in Cuba. From the exile side of the equation, the legal limit authorized is only $300 a quarter or $1,200 a year. A University of Florida (Gainesville) survey of one thousand arrivals in 1999 revealed that 61.3 percent received nothing from their families overseas and, of those receiving remittances in their households, only twenty nine, or three percent, received $200 or more per month, with 37.2 percent receiving US$100 or less monthly. This seems to indicate that an overwhelming majority of those actually making remittances comply with the law.

A survey of the income of Cuban exiles, published in March, 1996 in *Current Population Survey*, reveals that of 580,000 persons of Cuban origin gainfully employed 308,000 actually earned less than $15,000 a year. Therefore, even if we assume that all the ones exceeding those earnings, or 272,000, were sending remittances, the level of actual remittances would be closer to around US$320 million a year. A level of one billion dollars a year seems not feasible at all, since it will require 800,000 people sending US$1,250 yearly, which exceeds the pool of exiles earning any income.

On the Cuban side, the current exchange rate paid officially is around 26 pesos to the dollar. Therefore, a household receiving US$2,500 would have a yearly income in local currency equivalent to 65,000 pesos. This is quite in excess of the average income of army officers, policemen, medical doctors or university professors. The regime considers having relatives overseas a source of potential subversion. It would be highly unlikely that it would tolerate such a big proportion of people with overseas links having incomes so much in excess of what loyal members of the military or security apparatus, that is segment A, or members of the Party or other mobilizing organizations, segment B, are making. Therefore, the level of remittances must be substantially lower than the government reports, although even if it is only around US$300 million a year, it is still a significant amount.

From another perspective, the fact is that dollarization has ended the notion of class equality within the revolution. To cope with the problem of salary differentials between those working in state enterprises and in mixed enterprises with foreign investors, including the tourist industry, all kinds of ad-hoc arrangements have been made. Mixed enterprises are forced to recruit their staff from state companies and to pay the payroll in dollars to the company providing the staff. This company, in turn, pays the workers in Cuban pesos at the artificial exchange rate of one to one. This is equivalent to a confiscatory tax rate of almost 95 per cent. To overcome resulting protests ad-hoc arrangements have been made allowing partial payments in dollars. Dollar payments have been extended also to many state enterprise activities not related to foreign investors. A similar arrangement has been established to capture at least part of the tips earned by those servicing tourists.

Regardless of whatever convoluted efforts are made to compensate, the net result of dollarization has been the emergence of a privileged class with access to real buying power in dollars, quite in excess of that of the rest of the population, most of whom are limited to access only to peso income. This is the source of serious resentment within today's Cuba. As a result, special salary adjustments have been made to those in segment A from the MININT, as well as the MINFAR. Also they are given priority in the selection for jobs in tourism and dollar earning sectors of the economy. While this has brought a privileged status and differential in well-being to some people from segment A, it definitely is a source of irritation and dissatisfaction to those in the military and security forces left out, not to mention people in segment B and the rest of the population who are not able to benefit from access to dollar incomes, and therefore share the many hardships of those trying to live on a peso income.

Finally, it is worth pointing out there was a sixty percent decline in university registration, from 250,000 to 100,000 during the special period. Since professional salaries are paid in pesos, it is more rewarding to work as a bartender or a waiter in a restaurant for dollar tips than to practice a profession. This seems to indicate that access to university education is no longer an incentive to support the regime. As part of the educational reform undertaken by the government, university education has been extended to include extension and at a distance options, on a part time basis. This has resulted in an increase in university registration to 300,000.

Segment C includes many recipients of remittances, as does segment D. Two different reactions are present here. Access to remittances makes some people passive and unwilling to risk losing that privilege, while being free from regime pressure for their income makes others more willing to act independently and defy the regime.

Economic reforms constitute another internal event in the post-Soviet period that has had many repercussions on the attitude of various segments of Cuban public opinion. Faced with the collapse of an artificial economic relationship, the regime was forced to reorient itself to new markets even in traditional products first and afterwards to develop new products, as well as seeking new supply sources. New modes of management have been introduced in agriculture and industry, based on direct foreign investment and mixed enterprises, plus other forms of relationship of state entities with foreign partners. However, the opening suggested by reformers to allow Cuban privately owned small and medium enterprises was never instituted.

Self-employment was allowed in selected micro businesses, including paladares restaurants, taxis and room renting but, immediately after, regulations and heavy taxation were enacted to discourage their consolidation. In agriculture, cooperatives were created to manage large pieces of land but land ownership continues in state hands and most marketing of crops has to be done through state acopio agencies and acquisition of supplies through state controlled cooperatives. Control over independent agricultural producers has been reinforced by forcing them into state controlled cooperatives.

One success has been in expanding domestic oil production and reconditioning Cuban power plants to process the heavy oil Cuban wells produce. This has allowed Cuba to generate 90 percent of its electricity with domestically produced oil. The idea of generating electric nuclear power ended in an abysmal failure after all efforts to find alternative sources of financing and technology to complete the Soviet built Juraguá plant failed. Several hundred million dollars were lost and, according to rumors, this failure even caused the dismissal of Fidel's son from his post. Telephone service privatization has also been successful, as is the case of tobacco growing and cigar manufacturing and marketing.

Perhaps the most significant success has been the development of the tourist industry. Contrary to general impressions, investment in hotel facilities has been mostly financed by the Cuban government, to the tune of 95 percent, according to figures quoted recently in *El Nuevo Herald* from the Minister of Tourism at the Cancún meeting with US travel agents. Cuba is reaching almost 2,000,000 visitors per year. Foreign investors bring mostly operating capital and enter into management contracts, but actual investment in physical plant is done by the Cuban government, probably using money from money laundering since Cuba does not have surplus capital to invest. Ironically, in 1989, Castro executed general Arnaldo Ochoa, accusing him of being involved in a scheme of raising money from drug cartels to finance tourism investment.

Transportation between and within urban centers has practically collapsed. The housing deficit continues to grow and, shall a hurricane hit Havana, a substantial portion of the city may physically collapse. Despite all the investment in development of biotechnological plants, the supply of the most elementary medicines has deteriorated to a critical level, making moot the oversupply of medical personnel. Hospitals are reported to be short of the most elementary supplies, except those catering to the nomenklatura and tourists.

The final blow has been the reorganization of the sugar industry and the collapse in sugar production. The closing of 71 sugar mills has left more than a hundred thousand workers without employment and has had a devastating effect on the respective communities, the bateyes. These are small towns built around a sugar mill, that provide economic, social and public services, as well as a cultural life to many people beyond those actually working in the sugar mill. Closing so many mills in one single sweep has had an impact way beyond the immediate economic consequences of loss employment, etc. The government has tried to attenuate these consequences by keeping people in the payroll while they are reallocated, but this entails additional fiscal deficits and inflationary pressures.

As a result of these economic reforms, a new privileged class or oligarchy has emerged based on the military and security cadres who are given managerial positions in the state and mixed enterprises created by the regime. GAESA, or Group for Administering Enterprises, is a holding company operating out of the MINFAR to manage many such enterprises. Its president is Lieutenant General Julio Casas Regueiro, Raúl's right hand man and its operating officer is Raúl Castro's son in law. They bill around one billion dollars a year. Marcos Portal, the Minister of Basic Industry, married to a Castro niece, is claimed to have built another business empire. Another such conglomerate, specializing in tourism, is the holding company Cubanacán, billing more than US$300 million a year, whose top management was dismissed recently as a result of a corruption scandal involving the handling of dollar accounts. There are several other conglomerates or holdings that form part of this oligarchy that has emerged in the last decade. There are people from the military who are left outside and resent it very much. For example, General Menéndez Tomasevich, who at one time commanded troops in Angola, was one of those and asked for assistance in seeking exile some time before his death.

The impact of the reforms on the various segments of public opinion within present Cuba is diverse. Segment A is divided over the spoils being distributed by the Castro brothers. Some seek access to the benefits, while others resent being left out and have said so in communications with friends in exile. So, the will to resort to violence to defend the status quo is becoming contingent on the personal circumstances of those involved. Younger officers, both in the MINFAR and MININT are reported to be less committed to resort to violence to defend the revolution than those who perceive their fate is irrevocably linked to that of the Castro brothers, which is more likely to be the position of higher ranking officers. Nationalism should be assumed to be a motivation shared by all, which is the reason why Castro appeals to those sentiments with increasing emphasis. Segment B is less likely to share the benefits of the economic reforms and most likely joints the majority of the population in suffering the negative consequences of the collapse in the GDP, loss of employment and buying power in pesos.

Many of those people affected negatively from segment A and B have drifted to segment C, while others are seeking migration on so-called "quedaditos" arrangements, by which the regime allows them to live overseas and keep good relations with the regime, provided they are willing to pay some tribute from their income to government coffers and do not support exile opposition positions. Many Cuban doctors, actors and intellectuals contracted to work overseas fall into this category.

The economic reforms have created some economic space for segment D. However, those who try to use it may well be at the mercy of successive repressive efforts on the part of the regime. At this point, segment E continues to be an unrealistic alternative for people's responses. The repressive capacity of the state dissuades people from pursuing such an option, although increasing defiance of the regime and willingness to endure repression is a type of behavior that in some cases precedes resort to violence. If, as it happened in 1994 during the Malecón riots, frustrated people perceive a decline in the willingness to resort to violence on the part of segment A, segment E could explode with even more virulence than it expressed on that occasion.

The **emergence of the dissidence** is an internal event that has been underway since 1976, when the first organization was established to protest human rights violations. This process was greatly handicapped by lack of diffusion in Cuban media as a result of the monopoly of communications enjoyed by the regime. In 1985, this monopoly was broken by the inauguration of radio broadcasts to Cuba, the Radio Martí service under the VOA, during the Reagan Administration. Dr. Ricardo Bofill, one of the founders of the first human rights group in 1976 explained, upon coming into exile, that initially few people were aware of their existence, but once their activities were covered by Radio Martí, they were swamped by communications from all over the island.

The dissidence movement started growing in numbers as well as extended to many other sectors of activities beyond the denunciation of human rights violations. The regime has never been able, regardless of all efforts made, to bring the genie back into the bottle. Perhaps the most successful effort within the dissidence has been the emergence of independent journalists. Independent libraries have increased into more than a hundred, thus breaking regime control over what books people can read. Unions, farmer cooperatives, medical doctors, lawyers, educators, economists, and all types of NGOs have been formed to demand freedom of expression, assembly and association.

These organizations of the dissidence were usually small in number, a situation that led some people overseas to downplay their importance, not realizing that keeping membership small allowed better protection against the unavoidable and incessant infiltration of Cuban intelligence services. Even so, an association at a higher level of social organization was promoted when the meeting of Concilio Cubano was convened on February 24, 1996. Alarmed in the face of such an event, precisely on that day, Castro ordered the downing of two planes of the exile organization Brothers to the Rescue, which monitored rafters and boat people to guide the US Coast Guard to assist them. The four humanitarian pilots were killed in the downing by the Castro Mig planes over international waters. This brutal act was used as an excuse to cancel the meeting called by Concilio Cubano. One unintended consequence of this act of air piracy was the approval of the Helms-Burton legislation that up to that time had been bottled in conference by Senator Chris Dodd of Connecticut

But the dissidence survived that repressive action of the Castro government and continued to grow as people became disenchanted with the regime and realized the failure of the Communist ideology. More recently, the dissidence has survived the arrest and prosecution of 75 of its prominent members and, contrary to regime expectations, as was discussed above, has gained worldwide support, particularly in Europe and among the democratic left. Besides Payá's Christian Liberation Movement, the other dissidence organizations continue operating, the main ones being Vladimiro Roca's Todos Unidos (All United), the Asamblea para Promover la Sociedad Civil (Assembly to Promote Civil Society), whose President Martha Beatriz Roque is imprisoned, as well as groups headed by other leaders of the dissidence such as Manuel Morúa and Doctor Oscar Elías Biscet who was arrested separately and is being brutally mistreated in prison. They represent diverse ideological positions, but all share the commitment to a peaceful transition.

In terms of the various segment of Cuban public opinion, the emergence of the dissidence has created a valid alternative to channel personal actions for those who become dissatisfied enough to move from segments B and C into active, although peaceful opposition to the status quo in segment D. There is a circular effect, as people follow the advice of the Pope and lose their fears more of them join segment D. At the same time, the weakened regime tries to resort to minimum repression, aware of the negative image more brutal measures may generate overseas, while tolerating more moderate manifestations of opposition. Such hesitant repression fails to discourage the increasing unhappiness of those who are fed up. That is, those who have lost the fear of being afraid.

The regime is resorting to the practice of denying medical attention to prisoners of conscience in the hope that they will die of natural causes or be so weakened that, even if they are released, they will lack the physical and mental vitality to lead effective opposition efforts. But, at this stage, the willingness to endure repression seems to have hardened the victims of such despicable policies. Before too long, historical experience shows that, such tactics, will encourage many in segment D to start crossing the line and moving to segment E. That is, resorting to violence to oppose the status quo. Cuba seems to be reaching that situation.

The release of **La Patria es de Todos** in 1997 constituted an important event in the long run growth of a peaceful Cuban opposition to the regime inside Cuba, that is segment D. It was the first expression of a coherent ideology from a group from the dissidence, the so-called Group of Four. This document was issued in response to the comments of the Party to the program for the V Party Congress. It was the first time any group from the dissidence questioned the positions of the Party in relation to the past or the future. It strongly criticized the lack of freedoms and the fact that under the pretext of maintaining unity important decisions were taken without consulting the citizens.

The regime arrested the authors and, after a long delay, prosecuted them. This was a threat to the ideological monopoly of the regime leadership. It presented, for the first time, a coherent critique to government proposals and offered an alternative approach. It did not have too much impact on segments A and B, but it offered positions around which segment D could rally. The slow process of articulating a dissidence ideology had started.

The **Elian case**, and the so-called Battle of Ideas, was an internal event used very effectively by Castro to try to recoup the ideological initiative. By the end of the decade the ideological vacuum was evident to Castro. He was aware of the lack of revolutionary commitment among younger people. The new generation was alienated from the regime and this created a dangerous divide. The Elian case was an event used by Castro to revive revolutionary commitment.

With his swift perception of propaganda issues, Castro realized that a fight for parental rights offered him an opportunity to rally the population around the regime. At the same time, as the case developed, Castro realized it was also an opportunity to win support directly from the American people over the hated exile community.

To attain his dual objectives, Castro counted on the support of Dwayne Andreas, the top executive of ADM, the food producing and marketing giant that musters powerful lobbying powers in Washington. Andreas has an interest in Cuba in relation to ethanol, a gasoline additive in which his company holds a practical monopoly. Andreas has been trying to get the embargo lifted since 1995 and is the sinister force behind Castro's lobby in Washington that mobilizes American farm producers in support of lifting the embargo. To give an idea of Andreas integrity, or rather lack of, let us say only that his firm was fined $100 million dollars in a plea bargaining settling a prosecution, by Clinton's Justice Department, of violations of anti-trust laws and his son, Senior Executive Vice-President of ADM, was sentenced to two years in prison. The lawyer appointed to negotiate the release of Elian was Clinton's lawyer in the Monica Lewinsky scandal and also a partner in the Washington law firm that negotiated the above mentioned plea bargaining of ADM's anti-trust case.

The exile community had the naïve notion that invoking anti-Communism they could mobilize the American people in support of not returning the child to Castro. They did not realize that Communism ceased to be perceived as a menace by Americans after the demise of the Soviet Union. Meanwhile, Bill Clinton and Janet Reno used their contacts within the liberal American press to demonize the Cuban exile community with a most vicious racist campaign. Cuban-Americans were attacked with a ferocity that is unheard of in these days when such prejudiced treatment of any minority is considered to be not politically correct.

Championing the right of a father to be given control of his child became the rallying point of this campaign. And, that is an argument with which most Americans can identify. The fact that in Cuba children belong to the state and not to the family was ignored. And the fact that hundreds of defectors from Castro's regime are denied that right was also easily and conveniently overlooked. No American feminist came forward to argue the case of a mother who gave her life so her child could live in freedom.

The regime organized a campaign of protests in Havana and built a so-çalled "protestódromo" in front of the US embassy to be used in the frequent rallies, which Castro attended wearing his tennis shoes instead of boots. The whole campaign was wrapped under the banner of the Battle of Ideas, with frequent television roundtables and weekly rallies, "Tribunas Abiertas" throughout the island. Since, regardless of what segment of the Cuban public opinion spectrum they belonged, most people in Cuba could also identify with the cause of a father trying to recover custody of his orphaned son from exile relatives, the Elian case gave Castro a propaganda victory that he used to compensate for the loss of ideological identification with the revolution.

Eventually people got sick and tired of these constant mobilizations about a single issue, even if it involved a most charming young boy who became the poster child of the Cuban revolution throughout the world. The only unintended consequence of the Elián case for Castro was that Cubans in the island realized that the Miami exiles were not the Washington lackeys portrayed in Castro's propaganda.

The **Proyecto Varela** was another event confirming the consolidation of the existence of the dissidence as a long-term alternative to the existing order. For many years, Oswaldo Payá, leader of the Christian Liberation Movement, a group with unofficial support from the Catholic Church, has been trying to gather signatures to call for a referendum on opening Cuban society taking advantage of provisions in the 1976 Cuban Constitution. The Cuban secret police confiscated pages upon pages of signatures over the years to prevent Payá from attaining the required 10,000 signatures.

However, Payá was able to gather 11,200 signatures in support of a petition to hold a referendum and sneaked it into the Cuban legislature to present it formally. This fact alone indicates that there are people inside the regime who favor an opening as requested under the Proyecto Varela. In Cuba, no citizen has access to a public building without clearance from a very strong and effective security apparatus. And, with several boxes carrying thousands of signatures in support of a petition? It is highly unlikely.

Castro became very upset at this use of his own Constitution to challenge his totalitarian hold on Cuba's government. Borrowing from the techniques developed to mobilize the people under the Battle of Ideas, people were organized in marches to reject the petition. The "protestódromo" in front of the US embassy saw Fidel again in his tennis shoes leading marches. Millions of signatures were gathered ratifying the commitment to socialism and eventually the National Assembly of Popular Power, Cuba's legislature, was convened to ratify reforms to the Constitution making Socialism an irreversible component of the national basic law.

Payá got a big boost from Jimmy Carter's visit to Havana, during which Carter expressed support for the Proyecto Varela in his speech at Havana University in the presence of Castro. Internationally, the Proyecto Varela was also well received. The reason is very simple, for the first time the Cuban dissidence presented a proposal that was perceived as being willing to start from the existing reality and not seeking a return to the past, as well as not appealing to US support.

In essence, the Proyecto Varela proposes that a series of liberalizing measures be subject to a national referendum on which the people will be consulted. Among the measures involved are freeing of political prisoners, restoring basic human rights, such as freedom of speech, assembly, association, direct vote elections with more than one candidate and restoring the right to engage in private business, among others. The approach starts by recognizing that, within the existing Constitution, there are rights whose exercise the regime is denying to the citizens.

This is precisely the reason why there are people inside and outside Cuba who question the Proyecto Varela. They argue that, in fact, the Proyecto Varela recognizes the validity of the Communist Constitution which prohibits the exercise of any right that challenges the existing order, thus granting that Constitution a legitimacy it does not deserve. Castro's recent constitutional reform tends to make their argument even more valid, since it has made socialism and the one party state irreversible.

The important fact is that there seems to be a faction within the regime that realizes that the time has come to make an opening and are willing to engage people from the dissidence. It is logical to assume that those supporting these highly significant changes within the regime's inflexible ideological position belong to those in segments A and B associated with state and mixed enterprises who realize that the rigidity of Castro's stance is leading Cuba into a social explosion as the only way to attain change. A danger mentioned in La Patria es de Todos. Segment C is unlikely to care about the Proyecto Varela enough to come out of its paralysis. But, even this segment may welcome being granted a reduction in repression. And, definitely, a significant part of Segment D is supportive of this negotiated alternative. The fact that after the repression of dissidents in March, 2003, Payá was able to gather another 14,000 signatures indicates the widespread appeal of this option within segment D. On the other hand, several of the leaders of the dissidence, in and out of prison, led by Dr. Oscar Elías Biscet have recently expressed their rejection of any action predicated on acceptance of the existing Constitution.

The final internal event we will consider is **the Miami trial of Cuban spies**. The arrest of ten Cuban spies, known as the Wasp Network, took place on September 14, 1998, that is under the Clinton administration. They had been under FBI surveillance since 1995. According to an FBI Affidavit presented two days later, the arrest was made due to the interception of instructions to consider "the possibility of sabotaging planes and hangars at an undisclosed location in Florida."

The reaction of Castro was to immediately deny that he was involved in spying on US military capabilities and that the mission of the Wasp Network was limited to prevent exile actions against Cuba. There is ample evidence to the contrary. For example, in the FBI affidavit filed on September 14, 1998, the assignments of one of the spies infiltrated at the Boca Chica Naval Air Station in Key West was "to gather addresses of military personnel stationed at the base" among others. There is no way to relate this to gathering data on Cuban exiles activities. However, it complemented a report in the respected *Jane's Defense Weekly* of March 6, 1996 that Cuba was training commandos in VietNam to undertake attacks on American military bases in South Florida.

At that time, remember this was the Clinton era, the Pentagon was engaged in a project suggested by the head of the DIA 's Cuban unit, Ms. Ana Belén Montes, to promote relations between American and Cuban military. Retired American generals from the Southern Command, such as generals Sheehan and Wilhelm, started visiting Cuba under the sponsorship of a military think tank in Washington, the Center for the Study of Defense Information. Cuba created a counterpart center in the MINFAR to host these incredible new friends.

Two of these visitors, General Edward Atkeson and General Charlie Wilhelm, offered testimony in support of the Cuban spies at the trial. General Wilhelm justifies his testimony on being summoned by the defense. However, in his testimony, General Wilhelm went to the extreme of ridiculing the warnings he did receive from the FBI, after 1995, to tighten his security at the Southern Command with the explanation that the Cubans could not penetrate his counter-intelligence. What General Wilhelm did not know was that Cuban intelligence had penetrated the DIA and that the woman who came regularly from Washington to brief him on Cuba was actually working for Castro. This became public ten days after the 9/11 attack when Ana Belén Montes was arrested at her DIA office. She eventually entered into a plea bargaining which was settled in October, 2002, when she was sentenced to 25 years without parole in exchange for information on what she had done.

In terms of impact inside Cuba, the regime has tried unsuccessfully to convert the case of the Wasp Network spies into another case like Elian's. The five spies that went into trial--another five entered plea agreements--were eventually sentenced to long prison terms, to the surprise of Castro, who expected that the testimony of the generals would be enough to exonerate them. The jury obviously was more impressed by the evidence presented by the prosecutors, than by that of the generals.

The retired generals, however, continue to promote their relationship with the Cuban military and have supported a succession with Raúl Castro, once Fidel disappears. An idea planted by none other than Castro's spy at the DIA. As to Ana Belén Montes, Cuba has not allowed her name or history to be known by the Cuban people. Not one line has been published in Cuban media about her case. This silence is strange in view of her having acted out of sympathy for the Cuban cause and not for any financial gain.

Every week there are acts, Tribunas Abiertas, throughout the island honoring the "five heroes," as they are called in Cuban media, and a worldwide campaign has been mounted in support of them through organizations sympathetic to left wing causes. A Webpage has been created to register this worldwide support. The appeals made before higher courts in the US are constantly mentioned in the Cuban media with the argument that the trial procedures were faulty.

Within segment A, the impact of this campaign is limited to those who are aware of the failure of the generals to muster support of the Bush administration to pursue the same policies initiated under Clinton of endorsing a succession under the leadership of Raúl. Most people in segments A and B, however, do not have access to the background behind the campaign in support of the Five Heroes and are reported to be bored by it. People in segment C could not care less and those in Segment D are not familiar with the facts, so they are not influenced one way or the other.

All efforts to get the Justice Department to make available the information on the Ana Belén Montes plea bargaining and to publicize the damage assessment reports on what happened have met a wall of silence, making her case the less publicized one in the history of American betrayals. Perhaps, revealing what happened would be embarrassing to the CIA and the DIA or there are still agents out there being monitored who could realize they have been compromised if what Ms. Montes revealed is known. Maybe, there is a cover-up.

IV

POSSIBLE OUTCOMES

In view of the trend of events and the resulting deterioration of the external and internal situation, it is clear that the Castro regime is reaching its end. Besides, Castro´s health has deteriorated, and he is 77 years old. His brother Raúl, the designated successor, is 72 and his health is reported to be in even worse condition than that of Fidel. In this section we will consider the possible outcomes. Five outcomes will be discussed: A US intervention, a coup, a civil war, a succession and a peaceful transition.

In considering each outcome, we will consider two basic questions. One, how likely is it that it will occur? And, two, will it result in a satisfactory solution to the various groups in Cuban society that can result in a new stable situation? The answer to both questions will be framed in terms of the dynamics of the situation of the various segments of public opinion that is perceived exists today, as well as relevant possible future events. In addition, it is assumed that a stable situation is one that offers a reasonably satisfactory answer to the basic needs of the various stakeholders in the future of Cuba.

Four stakeholders have been identified in the future of Cuba: people from the present regime from segments A and B; people in the island from the opposition and the dissidence, that is, segments D and E; people from the exile community, that is overseas Cubans who are willing and able to participate in building a future Cuba and whose contribution could be critical to success in the reconstruction of the country; and, finally, the U.S government, which has basic interests in a stable future Cuba that it would be unrealistic to ignore and whose support or opposition would assure or deny stability to any outcome. It is also assumed that people at present in segment C, that is those indifferent or in a state of anomie, are unlikely to be active participants and, when relevant, their potential behavior in joining one side or the other as stakeholders will be noted.

Some will question giving any role as stakeholders to those involved in the present regime. That is unrealistic. And the military and security forces are essential to maintain internal order during that transition. Otherwise, Cuba's number one source of foreign exchange, tourism, could be placed in jeopardy. Cuba today includes a majority of individuals that, one way or the other, have been involved in the regime and it is impossible to discuss Cuba's future without including them. Others propose to exclude overseas Cubans or exiles as stakeholders. This is equally unrealistic from the other extreme. One of the irreversible demographic facts of life emerging from the Cuban revolution is the existence of a substantial Cuban diaspora, whose contribution and participation in the future of Cuba will be essential to its success.

Finally, super-nationalists on both sides of the Florida Straits, will object to the inclusion of the United States as a stakeholder. Again, the fact is that historical, economic and geographic factors make the US an indispensable actor in any successful reconstruction of Cuba. Even Castro, after his colossal mistake of trying to align Cuba with the Soviets ended in disaster, has been forced to base the Cuban economy on the dollar and to seek access to US markets for Cuban products and tourism. Granted, today there is a European Union, which has also a stake in Cuba's future, particularly Spain. Our brothers and sisters in Latin America also claim a stake but, as the historical record shows, they respond mostly to anti-Americanism, while remaining indifferent to the fate of the Cuban people. Still, our geographic location makes us part of the Inter-American System and our future is linked to the region.

But the future of Cuba cannot be based on chimeras. We have had enough of that under Castro. That is what makes the National Dialogue proposed by Oswaldo Payá so disappointing. Cuba cannot be rebuilt shutting out overseas Cubans, the US and contemporary trends. What is needed is an approach incorporating all stakeholders in Cuba's future and setting ourselves within what is happening today in the Americas and the world.

A **US intervention** is a most unlikely outcome, although there is substantial evidence that Fidel Castro has all along made preparations to cause an incident to force such a response from the United States. From the beginning of his regime, Castro has made comments indicating that the Cuban revolution will end in a war with the US. He has gathered intelligence and made military preparations useful for possible attacks on the continental US. He has built a network of contacts among minority groups in this country, which could be used to cause terrorist actions or riots that will arouse US public opinion in such a way that no administration could evade the option of resorting to an intervention in response.

The US response to such preparation has always been evasive rather than frontal, probably in order to avoid generating the pressure for the interventionist response. That is leading to a self-fulfilling prophesy. The problem with such caution is that, in dealing with somebody like Castro, and those around him, it may convey the mistaken notion of weakness or lack of willingness to stand up, thus feeding further aggressive behavior and even escalation.

After the initial hostile and aggressive US actions promoted under the Kennedy period, all subsequent administrations had taken limited stands on responses to security threats from Cuba, aware that an intervention could be a very messy and costly option. Not to mention the potential engagement of the Soviets escalating to a nuclear conflict. After the disintegration of the Soviet Bloc, Cuba has been downgraded as a strategic threat to the US. Three basic objectives of US security have been reported as being considered of priority concern in relation to a change of regime in Cuba: one, to avoid a massive migration to the US; two, to avoid being dragged into a civil war, should that occur; and, three, to reduce the danger of Cuba falling into such chaos that it became an easy base for the drug cartels using it as a corridor into the US. It was precisely on the basis of these three objectives that the Pentagon drew the mistaken conclusion, during the Clinton administration, that a Raúl Castro succession was the best option for the US.

Therefore, this outcome is highly unlikely to occur as a US imperialistic action, as portrayed time and time again by Fidel Castro in his rhetoric. Furthermore, with the passage of time, the option of provoking an incident leading to such an outcome becomes more difficult to implement for Castro. His charisma is losing effectiveness and implementation will require some MINFAR or MININT officer to follow his orders. The US could further discourage such officers from being willing to undertake provocative missions by making clear what the US response is likely to be. After 9/11, and the wars against Afghanistan and Iraq, such warnings from the US government certainly have credibility.

In any event, should an intervention occur, there could be a rallying of nationalistic sentiment with many people in segments A and B willing to give their lives for the defense of Cuba´s sovereignty, and even many from segments C and D. If there is one thing that Castro has accomplished is to awaken Cuban nationalism. If Castro is able to persuade the Cuban people that this is an unwarranted US action, people who are unwilling to die for Castro, will be willing to die for Cuba. There should be no mistake on that point.

A coup seems an unlikely outcome also, unless there is a social explosion or some event that totally overcomes the situation. The main reason is that Castro has created such a division of power within the military that nobody has command of enough forces to be sure he can control the situation without bringing so many people in that the conspiracy will be discovered. Besides, commands are rotated frequently to prevent the creation of personal loyalty cliques. And, military intelligence keeps all military leaders under close surveillance. There is no outside military power whose officers have contact with Cuban military officers to coordinate such an effort from outside. The Soviets no longer exist, the Russians have no credibility or influence and the US has had zero contact with line officers with command responsibilities.

To start with, within the MINFAR, the army is divided into three autonomous self-sustained regional forces, West, Central and East. In addition, there is a heavily equipped unit under direct control of Fidel Castro. The MININT has its own military capabilities, the Special Forces. This was a highly trained and well equipped force that played a central role in Angola. It was practically disbanded in 1989, as a result of the Ochoa affair, when its commander, Brigadier General Patricio de la Guardia was sent to prison and his brother, Colonel Tony de la Guardia, was executed by Castro. Recently Fidel Castro brought back one of his old buddies, Sergio del Valle, to reactivate the Special Forces unit. Furthermore, the Militia of Territorial Troops (MTT) is a reserve force formed by civilians which Castro can call to active duty to defend the revolution. The MTT was created in 1980, right after the invasion of Afghanistan by the Soviets in 1979, and its military capability is very limited, except that it would force any military leader of a coup to ponder the need to massacre many civilians to ensure control.

A coup would require a deterioration of the overall situation to a point at which military intelligence will cease to be effective and a spontaneous consensus would exist among commanding officers within segment A that Castro must be removed for their own self-interest. Segment B would be split under those circumstances between those still loyal to Castro and those wanting to join the military. However, all are likely to feel, and be, helpless in terms of having control of real forces to stand up to the military. Segment C is unlikely to be moved one way or the other. Segment D will be split between those, having some contacts within the military, who can try to join them to push towards a negotiated transition and those who would favor the total collapse of the regime. And, if there is anybody in segment E at the time, they are likely to raid bases and camps to seize weapons and attempt to take power, perhaps in alliance with people from segments A an B. This situation could degenerate into a civil war.

A civil war is equally unlikely as a first stage outcome. Although one could result in a second stage, if during the first stage the outcome threatens the basic interests of a significant portion of stakeholders from segment A. Of course, the regime can outlast its ability to maintain effective control of internal order if Fidel Castro attempts to stay in power beyond the period in which his charismatic authority prevails. If there is not enough public acceptance of Fidel's charismatic authority to grant the regime a minimum mantle of legitimacy, this will not work.

Castro came to power in 1959 when there was a tacit legitimacy granted to him by the Cuban people as the one who had offered the way out from the Batista dictatorship when all other options had failed. Then, his charisma took over as the source of legitimacy for the regime. Despite all the institutional trimmings, so far, there has been no institutionalization of that charismatic authority. Castro is the regime.

By prolonging his stay in power beyond any reasonable operational capability of the regime to attend the basic needs of the Cuban people, Castro could end eroding all the institutions of revolutionary Cuba, like Batista did in 1958 with republican institutions. If, under these conditions, there is a split in the command of segment A, a chaotic situation could develop in which all kinds of alliances between elements within segments D and E and A and B could emerge. At that point, it is unlikely that a civil war could result in an outcome in which one side emerges with enough power to attain the minimum legitimacy required to lead to a new stable situation satisfactory to all stakeholders.

In view of the current trends in public opinion, such a stable situation would require that a transition to a democratic regime be negotiated in which everybody's basic interests be guaranteed. And that will be extremely difficult to attain. The tourist traffic will collapse and the economy will shrink even more than it has during the Special Period. Since the country lacks financial reserves and stocks of food and other supplies the situation could turn chaotic and desperate. This is a most undesirable outcome for the Cuban people.

A succession outcome is likely to work only for a brief period of time as a first stage leading to a transition. And, even that would be feasible only if it comes while Castro still retains enough charismatic hold over followers and opponents to have his authority accepted. Raúl Castro has realized this and that is why he has stated twice in Cuban television that the US better try to come to terms with the revolution while Fidel is alive. He has a vested interest in that negotiation, because he is aware that, once Fidel is gone, he lacks either the legitimacy or charismatic authority to manage a succession.

Upon Fidel´s return from his trip early in 2003 to China and VietNam, Fidel indicated that he felt he will have to stay in power until he dies. Since then, Fidel never again mentioned Raúl as the successor. That could be either because of the deterioration in Raúl´s health or because Fidel did not like the Chinese solution that Raúl has advocated as a model for Cuba. Letting capitalists take over the economy, and even becoming accepted into the Party, are integral elements of the Chinese solution. Although Fidel expressed amazement at the material progress it had generated in China, that is not what he had in mind when he said he expected a continuation of the Cuban revolution under socialism after his death.

Whatever the reason, it was shortly after his return that repression of dissidents started in March, 2003 and that Ramiro Valdéz made a comeback from his retirement as having been twice Minister of the Interior. Ramiro was first appointed to the Council of State, the body--chaired by Fidel Castro himself--that rubber stamps legislation when the legislature is not in session, which is only twice a year for two days. Then, on July 26, 2003, on the 50th anniversary of the Moncada attack, Raúl was absent of all ceremonies and it was Ramiro Valdéz who gave the speech after Fidel. The next day Granma carried that speech in its front page in a box right under Fidel´s speech. That was a symbolic message of the status he had attained.

This must cause tremendous stress. Ramiro is known as an enemy of Raúl. Therefore, Raúl's followers within the nomenklatura have to feel threatened by the rise of such a man to a position as a potential successor. Ramiro is known as a brutal repressor and, like Raúl, has built a business empire, in his case around computers and telecommunications state enterprises. To people within segment A from the MINFAR, for Fidel to name his brother as successor is one thing, even if he lacks Fidel's charisma. But to name another individual, who also lacks his charisma, is a notorious repressor and threatens the future status of many officers from the MINFAR, must have raised substantial resistance.

Since those are the people who have been encouraging a pact with the dissidence, or at least with some among them, the personal attack on Elizardo Sánchez Santa Cruz is probably a manifestation of that silent struggle within the regime. This was a warning shot to stay in line and abandon any illusion of making concessions to the dissidence. Since these Raúl followers are too many to be given the Ochoa treatment, a warning shot at the expense of Elizardo is all that Castro can or wishes to do for the time being.

Outside of this struggle within segment A, that also includes elements from segment B, the succession could trigger all kinds of reactions in other segments of the spectrum of Cuban public opinion. Segment C is not likely to be initially too affected, although some elements within it may be motivated to move to opposition segment D if some of their interests are affected. Opposition segment D is likely to become more active, as well as to grow with the addition of people from segments A, B and C whose interests are threatened during the succession.

Opposition behavior is likely also to become more aggressive since during the succession the repressive power of the regime is likely to become more hesitant. And, hesitant repression usually fails to deter and feeds more resistance instead. Some elements of segment A, whose interests are threatened, are likely to move not to mere opposition in segment D, but to join segment E in resorting to violence to oppose the emerging new status quo.

In addition, this struggle among factions within the regime, in the presence of an obviously declining Castro authority over them, may result in a split within the new emerging oligarchy of managers of state enterprises. In fact, the recent dismissal and home arrest of the management team at Cubanacán has been attributed to Raúl as part of his fight with Ramiro, with whom this team was associated.

From these events it can be appreciated that not all stakeholders within segments A and B would have their basic interests attended under a succession. For segments D and E of the opposition and dissidence, a second stakeholder, there seems to be no concession at least so far. The overseas Cubans, another essential stakeholder in Cuba's future, are completely left out and the US is not likely to have grounds to lift the embargo, which under provisions of the Helms-Burton legislation, requires that neither Fidel, nor Raúl, be in power for that action to be taken.

Since the European Union has asserted its position of a democratic opening as a requirement for normalization of relations with Cuba, a succession without an opening will not qualify. This will not meet either the requirements for rejoining the OAS under the Democratic Charter, thus preventing Cuba, under a succession, from access to ALCA markets and IADB financing.

In addition, the experience of ten years of systemic transition in the Soviet Bloc, as reported by the World Bank, has shown that whenever an oligarchy of managers from the former regime retained control of state enterprises, the economic growth attained was not satisfactory due to continuation of state subsidies and inefficiencies. Therefore, a succession is likely to result in a continuation of the inefficient economic system that prevails at present in Cuba. This would lead, in the absence of Castro's charisma, to further strengthening of the dissidence and of their demands for concessions. The equilibrium between the regime capacity to repress and the willingness of people to resist and rebel could reach the critical point at which a social explosion will take place.

A transition is the final outcome to be considered. It seems it will be the only one capable to result in a new stable situation that meets the basic needs of all the stakeholders. As to the likelihood of it occurring, it seems that certain conditions and situations will be required, before that is possible.

The first step required for a transition would be to set up a roundtable with representation from people from segments A and B of the regime, from segment D and E of those opposing the regime, and from the exile community. The US Government has already established a Commission jointly chaired by Mel Martínez and Colin Powell to define possible US assistance to a Free Cuba. As was commented before, this Commission represents the leading, but not only foreign stakeholder in the future Cuba. It would be advisable for the US Commission to invite representatives of the European Union and the OAS, at the proper time, to join in planning that external assistance. The mere existence of such a broad based external arrangement to assist the future Cuba would in itself offer an incentive and a guarantee to potential stakeholders from segment A and B to see there is a way out of the present predicament for them.

The National Dialogue proposal of Oswaldo Payá, although reflecting a very narrow view of Cuba in isolation from overseas Cubans and present world trends, offers at least an initial step around which to start discussing a broader alternative within segments D and E. Overseas Cubans should start a similar process of setting up a Commission to consider the role they could play in assisting the reconstruction of Cuba. Great care and self-discipline will be necessary to ensure that such a Commission of Overseas Cubans avoids becoming a jumping board for political ambitions that would do nothing but threaten away people from segments A and B. One way to avoid that is to establish as a basic requirement for participation in the Overseas Cuban Commission, acceptance that the purpose of the Commission is to engage eventually in a conversation or dialogue with people inside Cuba, both from the regime and the opposition, and to articulate the assistance that could be provided by overseas Cubans to a peaceful transition. Consideration should be given by this Commission to the creation of an Overseas Cubans Development Fund to raise a pool of capital to channel to investment in Cuba's reconstruction.

The central objective should be to reassure the various stakeholders that their basic interests will be satisfied by the proposed transition. Segment A and B stakeholders in the future of Cuba need reassurance that their role is guaranteed. Neither the internal opposition nor the leadership of overseas Cubans may have enough credibility in offering such guarantee. These individuals in segments A and B have been conditioned to believe, as part of his charisma myths, that only Fidel's leadership protects them from US hostility. Therefore, guarantee of US acceptance of their presence in a regime, not including the Castro brothers, would assist in persuading many individuals in these segments to join a peaceful transition.

It must be realized that MINFAR and MININT cadres are essential to ensure that internal order will prevail, thus making the transition feasible. There is no other way to maintain law and order. It cannot be ignored that the most important Cuban industry today is tourism, which demands as a prerequisite the existence of law and order. It must be realized also that many in these segments may reject any such assurances, remaining Fidelista true believers to the bitter end. They will have to be isolated and dismissed from the armed forces or security apparatus. At the same time, efforts should be made to reduce these resisters to a minimum. The best way to avoid pushing them into resorting to violence is to assure them that their basic rights and interests will be respected. Finally, an effort should be made to avoid a Cuban piñata, a la Nicaraguan, in which a privileged group from segments A and B captures the majority of Cuban enterprises for themselves to the detriment of other Cubans, including, many within this segment.

The opposition in segments D and E is at present totally removed from access to any business undertakings, as are overseas Cubans, due to the present policies of not permitting private enterprises. A change of regime that does not make any provision to correct for that difference in starting situations will punish permanently those left out of access to ownership of Cuba's productive capacity. And, that includes many in the regime itself who have no access to the circle of privileged insiders. The transition must not only provide basic freedoms to the Cuban people but also make allowances that place all of them in a position to compete for a fair share of the future of Cuba.

In Cuba there has been a nationalization of all productive means to a degree never attained in any of the Soviet Bloc countries, a basic policy should be to end the role of the state as owner of the means of production and to privatize all of them. This will mean that the future Cuba will be based on private property as a basic principle in an uncompromising way. Therefore, the central initiative of a transition should be what in some of the former Soviet states was called a Massive Privatization Program (MPP): ***the national means of production should be owned by the people and not the government***. It must be clarified that this does not involve residential properties for which the principle of private property should also be restored, but should be handled in a different fashion taking into account the rights acquired by present tenants.

At present, the Cuban nomenklatura has been enlisted by the Castro brothers into a new oligarchy of enterprise managers to build support for their feudal regime. These enterprise managers enjoy only an uncertain status as hired managers of those enterprises, without any vested ownership rights. Any wrong move could end their tenure and status, as the cases of Ministers and managers removed recently demonstrates. In some countries in the former Soviet Bloc, the managerial cadres took over ownership of the enterprises under their responsibility by all kinds of devious means during the systemic transition. This led to unfair and undesirable consequences that hampered the reconstruction.

To reverse what the Castro regime has done, the ownership of the means of production could be allotted according to various bases.

Besides allotting a share to each citizen as owner of the Cuban state, the system for allocation should consider four groups of beneficiaries: manager and supervisory cadres, enterprise workers, to compensate former owner whose businesses were confiscated and to compensate those who were victims of repression or arbitrary actions from the regime, those guilty of human rights violations will be excepted. Certificates of ownership could be traded, thus creating a capital market outright. Managers and workers would have to pay the state over time for the certificates they are entitled to acquire, while victims of repression and confiscation will get their certificates free as compensation for whatever injustice they endured.

This is a most complicated undertaking and a study should be started immediately of the privatization efforts in the former Soviet Bloc to benefit from their experience. The World Bank has accumulated the most expertise in these matters and perhaps the U.S. Commission to assist a Free Cuba can request their cooperation.

This arrangement offers the option to the nomenklatura from segments A and B to change their present uncertain status as recipients of sinecures in exchange for supporting the Castro brothers, from which they could be removed at any time they displease their masters, into a guaranteed status of legal owners of a share of their enterprises. Workers would be assured a similar opportunity to benefit from the sacrifices they will have to endure to restore national wealth. That way every Cuban involved in productive activities will own a share of the future Cuba they will help create, instead of the present system that offers them only guarantee of contributing to create a bigger pie to be managed by the Castro brothers as they wish. Cuban workers have been denied adequate compensation for a long period of time and starting from the level of real income generated at present it is unlikely that their compensation would be satisfactory for some time. This way they would be sharing in the wealth being created for themselves and not diluted in the total national wealth under a state from which they have been denied the right to claim their share.

The issue of compensation for confiscations, both of national and foreign owners will be channeled into a process of documenting claims and sharing whatever is feasible to pay in current terms. Such a framework would automatically restore confidence in the respect for property rights, without which the massive investment required for the reconstruction, both national and foreign, would never be mobilized. Those who have suffered loss of freedom, torture and loss of relatives as a result Castro's policies could make claims to be compensated. And, in this group I include the hundreds of thousands of Cubans who were sent to fight overseas as part of the military service under the so-called "internationalist" missions.

At the proper time, the External Donors Committee headed by the US and the Overseas Cuban Committee can meet with those emerging from a National Dialogue to discuss the Cuba's reconstruction program and the role of everybody in implementing it.

A transition government operating under such a broad based system of ownership of the means of production would be able to democratize rapidly, respect all human rights and satisfy all the requirements of the European Union and the Inter-American Systems, under the Democratic Charter of the OAS, thus qualifying for access to the Cotonú Agreement, the ALCA, IADB and other international financial agencies. The transition would lead to an economic boom, instead of the chaos and tyranny offered by the succession outcome.

V

IS CUBA READY FOR A TRANSITION?

The previously discussed impact of external and internal events has brought Cubans on both sides to a moment of historical choice. It is highly unlikely that, in view of the external events that pressure towards a return to democratic rule as a precondition for being accepted not only by the US, but also by the European Union and the Inter-American System, any post-Castro leadership from segments A and B would consider feasible any outcome other than a return to democratic rule. The emerging dissidence that, even after the massive arrests of March, 2003, continues gaining force and popular support, has reaffirmed time and time again its commitment to seek a peaceful transition, free of any spirit of revenge. All are committed to democracy.

The only social framework that can provide the necessary guarantees for all sides is a return to a democratic system, based on the rule of law. Tolerance and respect for the rights of any minority that disagrees with the majority ruling the country are essential requirements. The sad experience of five decades of rule of hatred and repression, makes an overwhelming majority of Cubans crave for such a way out. Cubans want to be free of the "double moral", and they are doing so even in the face of regime repression. They also want to be free of the constant guilty feeling provoked by living illegally under the "resolver" culture all the time.

The regime has deliberately created an environment in which breaking the law is essential for survival and tolerance of scofflaw is a privilege that can be withdrawn at will by the feudal lord. People want to be able to meet their needs legally with money earned as a result of their work. No question bad work habits and a culture of ignoring the law will have to be overcome. But that has been done successfully in the systemic transitions in many former Communist countries

Every time Cubans, in the island or overseas, have been offered the opportunity of earning their living by taking initiatives, they have responded showing a remarkable spirit of entrepreneurship. Whether the recognized success of overseas Cubans, or the explosion of the "Mercados Libres Campesinos" in the eighties or "cuentapropistas" in the nineties, there is no doubt that entrepreneurship will not be lacking if the proper economic climate is created during the transition for a market economy to prosper. The artificial distinction between Cubans in the island and those overseas that is made to predict a meek recovery is not based on any objective evidence. Merely crossing the Florida Straits does not change the character of a people.

VI

OUTLINE OF TRANSITION ASSISTANCE PROGRAM

Having concluded that the most feasible and desirable outcome for Cuba is a transition, we can consider the international assistance that may be required. For that we draw on a previous paper prepared for the Cuba Transition Project under the title "International Organizations and Post-Castro Cuba." Here, only the last section of that paper is included, with the necessary adaptations to make it consistent with this monograph. For a discussion of the previous experience in systemic transitions that leads into the outline of assistance, the reader is referred to that paper.

The assistance program required from international agencies in the Cuban transition should be started in the pre-transition period. This has already been commented in a previous paper.[1] In essence, what is suggested is that the US Government, as the largest contributor to the IMF, the World Bank and the IADB, request from these agencies the formation of a preparatory working group or task force to start formulating a tentative program of assistance to Cuba during the transition. This request must be made by the US Treasury and the related costs financed through a grant from USAID. Since the present Cuban Government is not an active member of any of these organizations, there can be no formal objection from them to such a request.

At present, the Inter-American Dialogue is promoting cooperation between these agencies and the present Cuban Government, with a grant from the Ford Foundation. This cooperation is heavily influenced by the whims of the present Cuban Government, which allows or denies

[1] Betancourt, Ernesto F. Selected Technical Assistance Needs for Democratic and Institutional Transformation during the Cuban Transition, in Studies in Comparative International Development, Winter 2000, Vol. 34, No. 4, 60-61.

the participants from these agencies entrance to Cuba depending on the willingness of the Dialogue to submit to Cuban vetoes on who they may contact in other activities. For example, the project was suspended when the Dialogue invited CANF President Jorge Mas Santos to address one of its meetings. Under such a coercive atmosphere, it is unlikely that any serious research work can be undertaken. Besides, it is logical that the present regime will object to research related to a post-Castro Cuba.

But, even worse, there is a basic philosophical disagreement with the World Bank and the IMF which was clearly expressed by Castro himself during his speech at the Monterrey Summit on March 22, 2002, when he said that "their prestige is below zero," besides accusing them of promoting genocidal policies. The fact is that Castro rejects both neo-liberalism and globalization, two basic tenets of the policies of these agencies. Therefore, under present unofficial arrangements, staffers from these agencies going to Cuba end being mere props for Cuban propaganda efforts. Or, if they do any planning for assistance, they may have to renounce the principles that guide the stabilization and structural adjustment efforts of their agencies. In either case, what they are doing does not advance one iota preparation for transition assistance.

A. Preparatory work pre-transition assistance

Even under expedited procedures, it takes easily a year from the moment a country decides to apply for membership in these agencies to the moment disbursements start. Therefore, it would be advisable to consider other organizational options for these agencies to start the preparatory work required so that the time frame is collapsed as much as is feasible. The Helms-Burton legislation, under Section 202 (e) provides the basis for the US Government, through its directors at these agencies, to request that planning for assistance to a Transition

Government in Cuba be started by creating a joint preparatory working group or task force. Since the statutes of these agencies forbid using their financial resources in any work related to non-member countries, USAID can provide a grant to sustain such efforts.

The results of the preparatory work should be tentative plans contingent on the decisions to be made, at the proper time, by the authorities that emerge in a Transition Government in Cuba. The setting up of a flexible roll-over plan, properly sequenced in a computerized PERT system, should be one of the basic outputs of the preparatory stage. The recently created US Commission to Assist a Free Cuba seems the logical entity to request that international agencies start such preparatory work.

B. Emergency assistance

The first task that will require attention is the emergency assistance that will be needed to restore, from whatever is their deteriorated state, ports, highways, railroads, bridges, telecommunications and power generation. In this stage, supplies of food, medicines and spare parts to compensate from shortages in domestic output or imports will also be required. The World Food Program may also have to be involved but, since Cuba is a UN member and, in fact Cuba is at present a recipient of food assistance, it is not feasible for that agency to participate before an actual transition starts. Depending on how much progress is attained in preparatory work, USAID and other country donors are likely to have to provide financing for initial emergency assistance. The World Bank could schedule rapid disbursement balance of payment adjustment loans to reach effectiveness, or disbursement stage, as early as possible and emergency social fund programs to alleviate poverty and generate employment. IADB would also need to schedule emergency program loans, preferably jointly with the World Bank and other donors

[2] Quijano, Carlos N. "The Role of International Organizations in Cuba's Transition," paper presented at the Cuba Transition Workshop, sponsored jointly by Shaw, Pittman, Pott, and Thowbridge and the Association for the Study of the Cuban Economy, (ASCE), January, 1994, p. 5. This section will draw at large on this paper.

for early disbursement. The Transition Government should proceed to finalize access to the Cotonú Agreement and to establish the Framework Agreement for cooperation with the European Union, if they are still pending at the moment of the transition..

Assistance will be required in setting up a Round Table for transition preparation. As discussed above, it would be necessary to include representatives of the internal opposition and dissidence, of the suggested Overseas Cubans Commission and from segments A and B of the present regime who at the time are willing to engage in a dialogue for a transition. This work could be requested from the European Union, at the proper time, or from the Czech, Hungarian, or Polish Governments, as well as from Spain. If at all feasible, this should start during the preparatory stage. Cuba will also need assistance from the OAS in meeting democracy and human rights requirements as demanded by the Democratic Charter approved on September 11, 2001 in Lima, Perú.

C. Monetary stabilization

In these endeavors, the main focus will be on necessary changes in monetary and fiscal policies to move to a market economy, as well as to secure the financial assistance necessary to ensure currency and price stability. The IMF is the leading agency in such efforts, and membership in this organization is also a pre-requisite for being a member of the World Bank.

The IMF is the source of financing for stabilization agreements and also provides assistance in the formulation and administration of fiscal policies and of monetary policies and bank regulations. Such policies are crucial in attaining the discipline and encouragement goals of a successful transition to private sector development and competition. It also assists in restructuring foreign debt.

The Paris Club could play a role in helping the Transition Government deal with the foreign debt. The debt with the West, except the US which has none thanks to the embargo, was reported in Carmelo Mesa-Lago's presentation to the Association for the Study of the Cuban

Economy in 2001, to reach US$ 11 billions. Cuba also has a very large debt with the former Soviet Union that was surrogated to Russia and which Cuba has rejected. In settling this dispute, it should be demanded that the use to Cuban troops to promote Soviet interests in Ethiopia and Angola be recognized. Failure to solve this disagreement is one of the factors preventing progress in Cuba's efforts to reach an agreement with the Paris Club.

Parallel to these efforts, and complementing them to attain sound macro-economic management, would be those related to structural adjustment. The World Bank is usually the leading institution providing the policy and financial assistance related to the structural adjustment of an economy at the macro-economic level. This effort, in the case of Cuba, will have enormous ramifications. The IADB, as the leading source of international financial assistance in the Hemisphere, should share this effort with the World Bank. This means that Cuba will also have to join this agency, of which it has never been a member, and IADB membership requires the country to be a member of the OAS. Since Cuba's government is suspended from the OAS at present, the Transition Government will have to apply first to be reinstated in that organization.

D. Structural adjustment

In line with the lessons of transition in Eastern Europe, the central focus of the required structural adjustment will be attainment of a successful privatization that provides the framework for encouraging the emergence of a competitive market in which new enterprises flourish. It must, satisfy the aspirations of all internal stakeholders previously identified in the future of Cuba: those around Castro at present willing to join the future, the dissidence and overseas Cubans, and, of course, the people of Cuba in general. As discussed above, a massive privatization program will be the central issue around which to build a Cuba for all.

Structural adjustment will also require the enactment of new policies to ensure financial and market *discipline and encouragement* of entrance of new enterprises. In targeting poverty pockets and unemployment, complementary loans to a social emergency fund, that must be created, would be necessary. Assistance to social emergency funds usually involves other sources of financial assistance beyond the international lending organizations, including the European Union and country programs. The Overseas Cubans Development Fund suggested above could also become a contributor to the social emergency fund.

E. Productive and social sectors

At this stage, there will be some overlapping of assistance. Structural adjustment efforts will require, depending on the situation prevailing in the country at the time, that assistance be provided to cope with both productive and social sector problems facing the country. The IADB and the World Bank have developed many joint efforts in these areas in the Hemisphere and their joint experience will have to be drawn upon by the Transition Government. Therefore, both the World Bank and the IADB would be the leading lending institutions providing both, technical assistance for policy guidance and financing, for sectoral, productive and social rehabilitations or restructuring necessary to attain the required goals. The Overseas Cubans Development Fund could be one of the sources for financing sectoral and social projects, jointly with the international financial agencies.

F. State reform

Learning from the experience of the transitions in Eastern Europe, parallel to the policy changes there will have to be a massive reorganization of the public sector, as well as of the legislative and judicial apparatus, along with retraining of cadres in both the public and private sector. The organizational culture associated with the present regime will have to be replaced by a new one, as happened in

Singapore after independence, and was discussed in the previous study on selected technical assistance needs.[3]

Finally, a meeting of a Consultative Group should be convened to mobilize resources from external donors willing to participate in assisting the country, as well as private sector international banks. Cuba would be likely to attract many donors interested in participating in its reconstruction. As mentioned before, the World Bank, due to the wealth of experience it has accumulated on systemic transitions, would be the logical agency to prepare and manage the Consultative Group. However, the Inter-American Development Bank, as the largest source of financial assistance in the Hemisphere, may be preferred by the Transition Government.

To provide a map of all potential participants in the provision of assistance to the Transition Government in this extraordinary undertaking, a matrix has been prepared indicating the outline of the reform effort required in the Transitional Assistance Program and the potential role of the various international actors. As mentioned before, one the first assignment of the Preparatory Task Force or Working Group should be to establish a schedule for the assistance to be submitted to the Transition Government. Taking advantage of the lessons learned, institutional assistance for state reform, as well as training activities, should be scheduled parallel or preceding the proposed assistance for policy reforms. This will ensure that organizational structure and culture change along with the desired policy changes.

[3] Betancourt, Studies in Comparative International Development, p. 70.

TRANSITION ASSISTANCE PROGRAM ELEMENT	IMF	WORLD BANK
EMERGENCY AID		
Pre-transition planning	Participates	Leads task force
Infrastructure rebuilding and food, drugs and parts needs		Loan/ Rapid disbursement
Round Table	Cuba Rejoins	Cuba Rejoins, requires IMF membership
STABILIZATION		
Monetary and fiscal policy revamping consistent w/ market economy and macro-economic stability and Paris Club debt restructuring	Leads policy advice/provide short term financing/debt rescheduling	Participates and may provide loans for financial restructuring
STRUCTURAL ADJUSTMENT		
Advice on privatization policy, discipline and encouragement	Participates in reference to issues related to stability	Leads advice work based on transition experience and provides structural. adjustment loans
Social emergency fund created	leads or shares design advice and financing	leads or shares design advice and financing

)B	OAS	UN	EUROPEAN UNION	COUNTRY AGENCIES
'ticipates				US requests, AID finances
ın/ Rapid oursement		World Food Program	May participate	AID/FEMA
ɔa applies oin, requires S membership	Cuba Rejoins Assists on Democratic Charter		Cuba joins Cotonú and framework	Czech, Poland Hungary, Spain help set Round Table
'ticipates and y provide ns for ancial tructuring				
y share with Wold Bank vice work and uctural lending		UNDP or CEPAL may participate in advice work	May participate under Cotonú or Framework Agreements	Czech, Hungary Lithuania, Estonia may share their privatization experience
		May participate		Overseas Cubans & European countries may participate

TRANSITION ASSISTANCE PROGRAM ELEMENT	IMF	WORLD BANK
PRODUCTIVE SECTORS Assistance in restructuring under a privatized market economy, including advice and lending, for infrastructure, agriculture, small and medium enterprises, mining, domestic and foreign trade, etc.	May provide advice on banking reorganization and regulation	Provides sectoral adjustment. loans, alone or jointly with IDB,. others
SOCIAL SECTORS Assistance in restructuring, in accordance with a market economy, provision of health, education, housing, etc.		Similar role to the one on productive sector reform
STATE REFORM Consistent with above policy revamping, assistance for a massive change in public sector organizational structure and culture, including executive, legislative and judicial branches	May provide assistance in fiscal policy formulation and management	Assistance in modernization of the state and the judiciary
Organization of Consultative Group Meeting to ensure effort coordination and pledges of resources.	Shall participate	Should lead due to transition experience

B	OAS	UN	EUROPEAN UNION	COUNTRY AGENCIES
vides toral loans, ne or jointly n World k and oth-		May provide assistance through UNDP, CEPAL or UN agencies	May provide assistance under Cotonú or Framework Agreements	Each country agency will select areas for their participation. Overseas Cubans Fund may finance
ilar role to one on ductive tor reform		Similar role to the one on productive sector reform	Similar role to the one on productive sector reform	Similar role to the one on productive sector reform
y take lead assistance f/ dernization the state, legislature d the iciary	May provide assistance in human rights, legal reform, w/ Democratic Charter and elections	May provide assistance through UNDP and CEPAL	May provide assistance through the Cotonú or Framework Agreements	AID can provide assistance for electoral system. Others, according to their priorities
all ticipate, d alternative	Shall participate	Shall participate	Shall participate	Shall participate as required, including private banks and ONGs

APPENDIX

I started working on this model while representing the 26th of July Movement in Washington back in 1957 and 1958. At that time, I did not receive any instructions on the positions of the Movement in relation to events; yet, as their spokesman, I was required to state our position to the Washington press. And, this had to be done in a timely fashion.

To cover that gap on the social theory side, I first went to The Library of Congress and read all the books available on analysis of revolutionary processes. I read some classical books on the sociology, psychology and natural history of revolutions. I also bought Crane Brinton's *The Anatomy of Revolution*, which at the time came out in a paper back edition. It was also widely read by Cubans in those days.

Perhaps more to the point. Parallel to this search for theoretical knowledge, I started searching for all indications of Fidel Castro's positions, not only from his statements but also from those who were coming to Washington who, one way or the other, knew about his thinking on the various relevant questions and issues. This was the beginning of a lifelong effort at Castro mind reading that continues to this day. To use a very ugly word, I became a Castrologist.

The FBI watched my activities at the time and informed me that I had to register as a foreign agent at the Justice Department, which I did. From time to time, they will come to talk to me and, on one occasion, they raised the issue of how I was getting instructions on what position to take in my press releases. They assumed I had some super modern communication system to reach Castro in the Sierra Maestra. When I explained how I did it, they were skeptical. My only risk was that, if at any time, I issued a statement that was repudiated by Castro, my credibility will be finished. Fortunately for me, this did not happen at any time during the two years I acted as Washington spokesman for the Movement.

In fact, the results of my analyses, informal as they were, made me feel confident enough to take the decision on November 15, 1958 to resign, effective January 1st. 1959, my job at the company where I earned my living and rearrange my family affairs so that I could devote all my time to the revolutionary cause.

After the defeat of Batista, I was able to enrich my personal appreciation of Castro's views through a more personal interaction. On April 1959, I was asked to accompany Castro in his visit to Washington as his advisor on the US political establishment and the issues that were relevant at the time. Castro ordered that I be lodged next to him throughout the trip and I had the assignment of waking him up every day at 6:00 AM, regardless of at what time we had gone to bed. We then discussed the issues of the day on a unique one to one basis. This allowed me the opportunity of further observing how he reasoned and reacted to the issues that came up.

Afterwards, upon our return to Cuba, I persuaded Castro to arrange for a weekly meeting with the economic cabinet at the Banco Nacional and to set up the Tourist Development Board, which he presided and I coordinated. This gave me further opportunities to observe how he reacted. By the end of the year, I had had enough and resigned when Major Hubert Matos was arrested and Che Guevara became President of the Banco Nacional. Shortly after, I returned to Washington.

It was precisely by making an analysis of revolutionary propensity that I reached the conclusion that the Bay of Pigs expedition was doomed to fail. Even if the US military had been ordered to provide air cover and land at the last minute by President Kennedy, as was the plan of the Joint Chiefs of Staff at the time, the invasion was going to be a historical disaster. I had no doubt that our side would have eventually prevailed. But the cost would have been terrible, both for Cuba and the United States. In my opinion, although Kennedy was trivial in his approach to the operation, both Cubans and Americans should be grateful for his having had the courage to take blame for the failure and stop it, rather than compound the historical mistake made.

I was one of the very few people who opposed the operation and, through my friend Charles Bartlett, who in turn was a close friend of the new President, almost stopped it. All I got as a result, however, was an accusation from Allen Dulles of being entangled with a pro-Communist group. Such accusations could not be taken lightly in 1961 Washington.

When, many years later, I was appointed the first director of Radio Martí, I decided to make a more formal presentation of the methodology to share it with my staff. For that, I drew on notes I had prepared for lectures at the University of Pittsburgh and a graduate seminar I led one semester at Georgetown University. The logic behind Radio Martí was, and still is, that, in the end, political changes require changes in public opinion, starting with being informed. Revolutionary changes, involving as they do resort to violence, require the most intense changes in the attitudes of the people involved on both sides of the conflict. That is, going from those willing to resort to violence to maintain the status quo to those willing to resort to violence and endure repression to change it.

After I left Radio Martí in 1990, I decided to formally publish in book form the notes I had prepared for the orientation sessions I gave to Radio Martí staff members. I also wrote two applications using the methodology I had developed, one, to explain how Castro defeated Batista and, the other, how the Tupamaros failed in their revolutionary efforts in Uruguay. I was encouraged to write this book by my good friend, the great sociologist Irving L. Horowitz, who had it published by Transactions Publishers in 1991,under the title: *Revolutionary Strategy: A Handbook for Practitioners.*